Life in the Amazon Rain Forest

by Ronald Scheibel

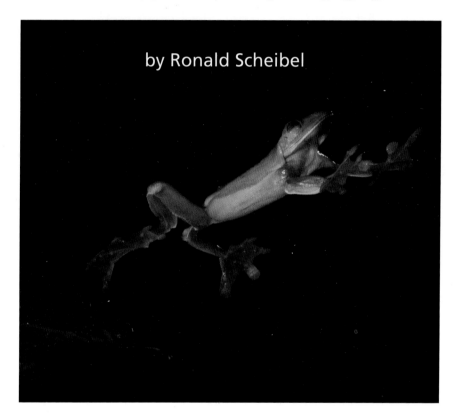

Glenview, Illinois • Boston, Massachusetts • Chandler, Arizona
Upper Saddle River, New Jersey

Life in the Amazon Rain Forest

Think of a big building with many floors. The Amazon rain forest is like that.

The rain forest has four levels. Each level is a different habitat for the things that live there. Many animals and plants live at each level. The four levels are:

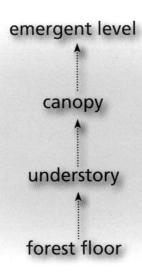

emergent level

canopy

understory

forest floor

The Rain Forest

It is very wet in the rain forest. It is also very dark. Tall trees grow there. Their thick branches block the sun.

Near the ground, the trees spread out like fans. The soil is not very deep. The big roots of many trees hold on to the ground.

Big tree roots keep the trees from falling.

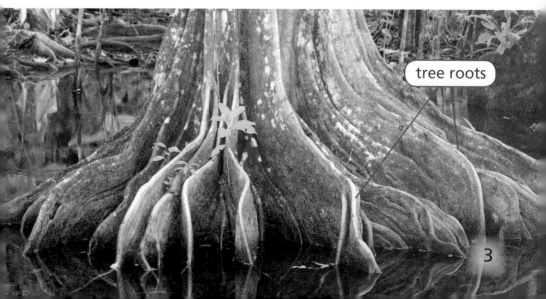

tree roots

The Forest Floor

On the ground, you can hear birds and monkeys call out. Insects buzz and crawl.

Leafcutter ants live in big groups. Their nests are underground. The nests can be as large as your classroom.

The ants take leaves to their nests. Fungus grows on the leaves. The ants eat the fungus.

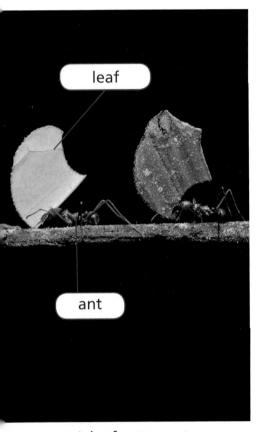

leaf

ant

A leafcutter ant
hard at work

The Understory

The understory is the level above the ground. Smaller trees and plants grow here. Some plants grow on tree trunks. They have no roots in the ground.

Big spiders called tarantulas live here. They eat frogs, lizards, and birds.

tarantula

Tarantulas can be ten inches across!

Some bats live here too. They drink from flowers. They also carry pollen. This is good for the bats and the flowers.

opossum

Monkeys and
opossums
share a home
in the canopy.

The Canopy

The canopy is more than 100 feet above the ground.
Tree branches block the sun. Monkeys jump from tree to
tree.

The canopy is busy. It is crowded. Some animals
share homes. Monkeys sleep at night. Opossums sleep
during the day. They share a home because they sleep
at different times.

The Emergent Layer

The emergent layer is at the top. The trees are more than 130 feet tall!

The emergent layer is the driest layer. Here, you can see the sun. You can also see tree frogs. They glide up to 40 feet! There are more than 1,800 kinds of birds. There are more than 250 mammals here too.

Welcome to the beautiful world of the Amazon rain forest!

The tree frog glides through the air.

frog

The Four-Level Rain Forest

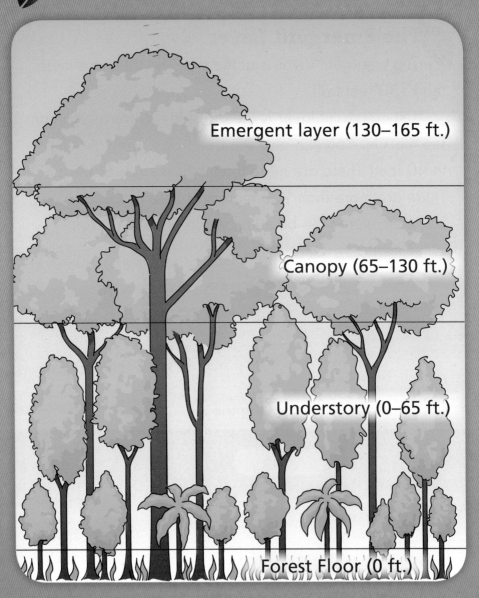

Emergent layer (130–165 ft.)

Canopy (65–130 ft.)

Understory (0–65 ft.)

Forest Floor (0 ft.)